The Haunted

Written and Illustrated by

John Ryan

One day Mr Noah put up a notice outside his cabin to show that he was busy.

He and Mrs Noah were spending the day looking after their flowers and vegetables and planting new ones.

Jaffet their youngest son and his friend Jannet were looking after all the animals that Mr Noah had brought on board the Ark.

Crockle, their pet baby crocodile, was with them.

Ham the second son
was doing odd jobs

and Mrs Ham was cooking
a super soup for supper.

As usual, Mr and Mrs Shem
were checking the food stores.
They checked the stores
every day

and they did it very, very carefully.

'But there ought to be six thousand four hundred and thirty!' cried Shem. 'There are five potatoes missing!'

'That's not all, Shem,' said his wife. 'There were *four* onions missing yesterday and *six whole broad beans* the day before!' 'You realise what this means,' said Shem. 'It means that one of the animals is stealing food! We must send for the children. Because,' he added darkly, 'I expect it's that baby crocodile of theirs!'

Now Crockle shouldn't have been on the Ark at all, because there were already two perfectly good (or bad) crocodiles on board. But the children knew he wasn't a thief. When they arrived, they said so to Shem.

'In that case I shall have to question all the animals,' replied Shem severely. 'Call them together in the central hold. I must get to the bottom of this.' Just then, Ham came along. 'It seems a lot of trouble over five potatoes,' he said. 'Have you told Father Noah?'

'He's busy,' said Shem, pointing to the notice on his father's door. 'Don't worry. I can handle this.' Meanwhile the children were collecting all the animals.

DO NOT DISTURB

When they were all there Shem told them what had happened. 'This is a serious matter,' he said. 'If the guilty animal doesn't own up,

there will be no more sugar lumps on Sunday!' And he looked hard at Crockle. The animals were very shocked. They loved their Sunday sugar lumps.

Some looked suspicious . . . and some looked innocent.

The crocodiles looked almost too good to be true!

And *all* the animals turned to Crockle.

But no one came forward to own up. 'That's it then!' announced Shem. 'No more sugar lumps until we find the thief!'

The children looked at each other in dismay. 'This is bad,' said Jaffet. 'Of course we know Crockle didn't do it. But Shem thinks he did and so will all the others unless we can find the real culprit.' 'And the animals do so love their sugar lumps,' said Jannet. 'What can we do?' 'I know what,' said Jaffet.

'Let's guard the food store tonight. Maybe the thief will come back. If he does we'll catch him red-handed.' 'Or red-pawed,' said Jannet.

So that night Jaffet and Jannet and Crockle crept down to the food store. There was a light under Mr Noah's door but everyone else was fast asleep.

The children could see quite easily. There were night-lights everywhere in case any of the animals were afraid of the dark. But when they got to the store . . .

it was very dark indeed and there were long black shadows everywhere.

Jaffet held up his candle. 'That's better,' said Jannet. 'But it's very creepy down here! Do you believe in ghosts?' 'Of course not,' replied Jaffet, 'I feel more sleepy than creepy!'

Just then there was a loud noise right next to them!

Both children jumped and Jaffet almost dropped the candle.

Then they saw what had happened. Crockle had been sniffing round the store. And somehow he had managed to tip over a barrel of apples and then fall head first into an open flour bin.

When they lifted him out of the bin both children burst out laughing. Crockle looked so funny! He was covered all over in flour and gleamed white from top to toe. 'You look just like a ghost, Crockle!' said Jaffet.

Then Jannet said, 'That's given me an idea. Why don't we make a booby trap for the thief?

'We'll balance a sack of flour on top of the door. If any animal comes in, the sack will fall on him and cover him with white. Then even if he gets away we'll be able to tell which animal it is!' 'That's a super idea,' said Jaffet.

So they chose the biggest sack of flour they could find. Jannet climbed up and fixed it on top of the door. They left the door a little bit open. Just as they finished they heard a sound outside.

It was Shem. He'd been woken by the noise Crockle had made and thought the thief was in the food store. So now *he* was on his way down to catch him. But of course the children couldn't see who it was. 'Quick! Blow out the candle!' whispered Jaffet.

'There's someone on the stairs!'

thought Shem as he pushed open the door.

And someone did!
It was Shem!
Because the children's
booby trap worked
very well!

Down came the sack on to Shem's head. He was covered from head to foot in flour!

'Help! Robbers! Fire! Murder!' he cried, and ran for his life back up the stairs. 'Oh dear!' said Jaffet. 'That didn't sound like an animal!'

'It sounded like your big brother Shem,' said Jannet. 'And that means trouble,' answered Jaffet. 'Come on. We'd better go after him!'

But they were too late to catch poor Shem. He couldn't see where he was going but that didn't stop him. He was still shouting when he dashed into the animals' quarters.

The animals woke with a start. They took one look at the ghostly white figure of Shem . . . and bolted!

The noise of the animals stampeding roused Mr and Mrs Ham. And when they saw what was happening and heard all the roaring and howling and screeching, they ran for their lives!

Then Mrs Shem woke up. She saw her brother- and sister-in-law running towards her with all the animals behind them. In a flash she was out of bed too, and away!

So now Mrs Shem and Mr and Mrs Ham and all the animals were on the run.

Out of one door on to the deck they ran with the ghostly white figure of Shem chasing them, and Jaffet and Jannet and Crockle chasing Shem.

Round and round the deck they all rushed howling and growling, roaring, barking and shouting. Then inside again, and up the stairs to Mr Noah's cabin.

What on earth is happening down there?

Mr and Mrs Noah were still busy looking after their plants. They were *very* surprised to see so many animals and people. And when Shem and Jaffet and Jannet and Crockle arrived Mr Noah cried, 'What's going on? Why are you covered in flour Shem? Take that ridiculous sack off your head at once!'

By this time there was such a crowd in Mr Noah's cabin that the larger animals had to go back to bed. Then Mrs Noah said kindly 'Now calm down everybody and tell us what happened. Then we'll all have a nice cup of tea and settle down for the night.'

So the children told all about guarding the food store and Crockle and the booby-trap.

And then Shem told them all about the missing food.

Mr and Mrs Noah both roared with laughter. 'If only you'd told us!' said Mrs Noah. 'It was *I* who took the potatoes and onions and beans . . . *to plant them!*'

'It was all my fault,' said Mr Noah. 'I shouldn't have put up that Do Not Disturb notice. No wonder the poor animals were frightened! Let's give them all an extra sugar lump now!'

'Starting with Crockle,' said Jaffet. 'He still looks a bit like a ghost himself!'

So the animals all had a bed-time sugar lump and then everyone went off to sleep.

But no one ever forgot the night the
Ark was haunted!